"Unless a man understands the Weald, he cannot write about the beginnings of England."

Hilaire Belloc

Published in the UK in October 2015 by Champaign Publishing to accompany the exhibition of paintings "Between the Downs".

ISBN No 978-0-9926263-1-0

Design: Neil Haggar
Printed by: SRP, Chichester, West Sussex PO19 8TU

Also by Champaign Publishing:
"The Road to Kandahar"
Published 2013

Katimavik, Durfold Wood,
Plaistow, West Sussex RH14 0PL
Tel: 01483 200456

WINDOW ON THE WEALD

SCENES & STORIES

Champaign Publishing

MY WEALD

By Richard Pailthorpe, Director of the Weald & Downland Open Air Museum

It's a panorama that has inspired and intrigued locals and visitors to the South-East of England for generations and, as the head of an organisation that literally has its foundations derived from the Weald, I am grateful for the opportunity to contribute my own snapshot of this marvellous landscape.

Its two distinctive geological areas comprising the Weald and the chalk Downland to its north and south form a countryside patchwork of quintessential English villages with historic churches and village greens, isolated farmsteads, small pasture fields surrounded by hedgerows and narrow woodland belts known as "shaws", hammer ponds and meandering streams.

The central High Weald with its sandstone ridges, outcrops and steep-sided ravines called ghylls is a designated Area of Outstanding Natural Beauty. The Low Weald, is a low-lying clay vale bordered by a belt of greensand and clay. It stretches from the eastern boundaries of Hampshire across central Surrey, Sussex and Kent.

The name "Weald" is derived from the old English meaning "forest" and during the Saxon period it was known as Andredeswaeld or the "forest of Anderida", the Roman name for Pevensey. The forest though provided a vital natural resource of timber for numerous industries which were developed around it. The oak was the predominate forest tree and became known as the "Sussex Weed".

The traditional forestry economy was based around harvesting a mixed coppice of hazel and chestnut with oak standards, which provided the timber for ships and buildings. The young wood and coppice supplied the fuel for charcoal to fire the kilns for smelting iron ore or glass furnaces, as well as being the raw material for many by-products such as wattle panels for use in buildings, sheep hurdles for farmers, fencing or making the famous Sussex trug.

The Weald probably has the richest resource of timber buildings and building styles to be found in the country. Weather-boarded cottages, comfortable manor houses constructed of local sandstone and often roofed with giant slabs of Horsham stone together with brick-built Georgian houses make up the rich diversity of the built environment.

The particular "Wealden" house style developed during the 15th Century is associated with the rising class of yeoman farmers and successful merchants of the period. Bayleaf Farmhouse at the Weald & Downland Open Air Museum in West Sussex is a fine example.

Rescued from the site of the Bough Beech Reservoir,

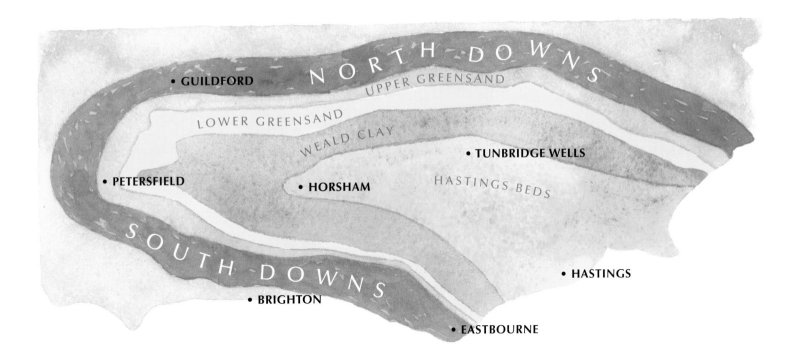

near Chiddingstone in Kent, it has been painstakingly rebuilt and furnished to show how it and a typical Wealden farmstead may have appeared during the early 16th Century.

Small remnants of the ancient Wealden Forest survive such as the Mens Wood, near Petworth in the West Weald. Other reminders such as St.Leonard's and Worth Forests and notably Ashdown Forest can also be found. The latter is the largest area of heathland in the South-East and was formerly a medieval royal hunting forest surrounded by a pale fence to enclose the deer. Hunting was a popular pastime in the middle ages and a number of deer parks and rabbit warrens were established.

A network of sunken lanes and byways throughout the Weald owe their origin to livestock being seasonally moved in search of new pastures along droveways from the coast and the Sussex hinterland. Today's breed of Sussex Cattle are direct descendants from those used as oxen to pull ploughs to cultivate the land, a practice that continued in a few places until the turn of the 20th Century.

The primary contributory reason for the destruction of the forest was the Iron industry. Iron smelting had taken place for centuries on a comparatively small scale. However, it was during the 16th and 17th centuries that the industry made the Weald the industrial heartland of England. Forges and water-powered charcoal blast furnaces producing cannon, together with hammer ponds became a feature of the landscape, which with glass making competed for the diminishing supply of timber. Finally, by the early 18th Century the discovery of coking coal led to the industry moving away from the South-East, although the last furnace did not close until 1809.

The Wealden forest with its heavy clay soils was for centuries considered an impenetrable obstacle for anyone travelling across the region, and in effect cut off the Channel coast from the rest of the country. The reputation and condition of Sussex roads "full of dirt and myre" was notoriously bad, but by the mid-18th Century with the introduction of the Turnpike Trusts the situation began to improve.

Along with an improved road system came the introduction during the early 18th Century of canals, linking the Sussex coast with London, via the Wey-Arun canal- "London's lost route to the sea".

However, the coming of the railways by the mid-19th Century heralded the decline of the canals and the rapid opening up of the Weald to London commuters and the tremendous development pressures it continues to face today.

The National Trust, Wildlife Trusts, the RSPB and numerous private and charitable organisations help to conserve the region's historic and unique landscape.

A special feature of the central Weald is its many beautiful gardens include Wakehurst Place, Nymans, High Beeches, Borde Hill, Great Dixter and Sissinghurst.

But what does the future hold for this special part of the UK? The Sussex landscape became a popular cause for concern with public attention being drawn to the threat of development and the destruction of the countryside after World War I.

Conservation is key to the future and faced with an ever-increasing demand for housing, the expansion of air traffic from Gatwick Airport and other 21st Century demands such as oil exploration, the Weald faces many new challenges.

But here is an ancient and living landscape which still fosters the traditions and cultural heritage of its fascinating past thus providing a bedrock for the eventful years ahead. ■

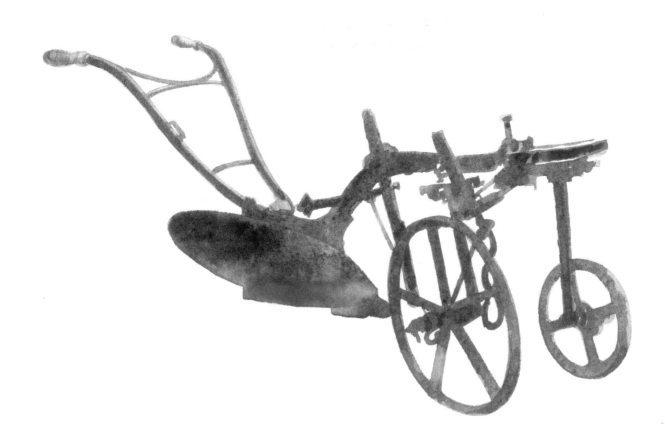

CONTENTS

Field Edge, Blackmoor   *Watercolour*

THE WONDERFUL WEALD

The Weald, an oval-shaped area covering more that 1,000 square miles between the North and South Downs, has hidden its many charms for centuries. Indeed it has been said that this natural marvel is "famous for not being famous".

Until the 1950s it was one of the slowest changing regions in Britain but inevitably the framework of life has altered to meet the demands of modern living.

The ancient, untamed oak forests no longer provide the charcoal from the woodlands that supplied the furnaces and forges of the ironworks which formed an important industry in the south.

Farmers who for so long had worked with nature to produce crops and livestock now face unprecedented pressure as a result of soaring land values, competition from cheaper, imported products and changing consumer preferences.

However, the Wealden landscape has not been lost to increased mechanisation and mass production. Its natural beauty, cultural traditions, small farms, compact fields, real hedgerows and green lanes have survived.

Some say that the Weald is more closely associated with fiction rather than fact. And it is easy to see why when looking at the prominence of its near neighbours – the designated national park to the south and the areas of outstanding natural beauty among the ridge of chalk hills to the north. But that is not to say that such recognition has escaped the Weald which has its own area of outstanding natural beauty within the High Weald.

Life and working practices are changing within the Weald but not at the same pace as elsewhere and the landscape is still more a product of traditional farming techniques than intensive operations.

Charcoal burners can still be found in the woods, village life still retains many of the values and customs of yesteryear and evidence can still be found of industries such as iron working and glass making.

Poets, writers and artists were inevitably drawn to such a nascent part of the country and there exists an international body of work inspired by life in a region that occupies the greater part of Kent, Surrey and Sussex with a fringe of Hampshire.

"Window on The Weald" captures in words and paintings some of the past and present day activities that make the Weald such a compelling and rewarding study for anyone interested in a diverse countryside of sandy heathlands, rich loams, chalklands and tidal marshes.

It is a snapshot of the countryside and the characters within, a tale of the famous and the infamous, an illustrated explanation of past and present wonders of the Weald.

The book's creators are international landscape and wildlife painter Gordon Rushmer who has worked as a professional artist for over 45 years from his home in the Weald, and writer David Holmes who has accompanied Gordon on many of his travels in search of the intriguing, the inspirational and the unexpected. ■

Hampshire Winter   *Watercolour*

January Day in the Kentish Weald   *Watercolour*

With such an abundance of natural features, any season in the Weald offers an ever-changing tapestry of scenery and sensations.

Swathes of cultivated land are interspersed with thick blankets of forest and heathland. Natural wildernesses add drama and comfort in equal measure as the stark, isolated beauty of such wild lands lead downward to pockets of habitation and signs of human activity.

In such wild places, it is not difficult to imagine what life was like in the Weald in days gone by.

In winter the pace of life slows in preparation for the plummeting temperatures, dramatic frost formations and the occasional covering of snow that mutes the green and brown surfaces with a crisp, white covering.

Loves Farm, Easebourne   *Watercolour*

Morning Mist, Longmoor   *Watercolour*

Ashdown Autumn   *Watercolour*

Apart from the more exceptional snowfalls, life carries on as normal in an area where humans, animals and plant life adapt to the forces of nature.

Spring brings a multi-hued carpet of bluebells, daffodils and other harbingers of the warming touch of summer when growing conditions are at their peak for everyday and exotic species.

As summer moves on, the fresh bright greens become dull and even "sooty" – colours that artists find so difficult to translate onto canvas.

The coming of autumn dampens down this activity but not before the burst of vivid reds, yellows and russets in the fields, forests and hedgerows.

Each season is special and highlights the diversity and divergence of city and rural life, a point well made by author and poet G K Chesterton in "The Old Song" when he wrote that the Weald was "the place where London ends and England can begin."

Capturing the transient beauty of Mother Nature has been a preoccupation for artists for centuries. Some specialise in a particular aspect such as the study of birds, flowers or scenery with their work expressed in many different mediums - photography, woodcuts, watercolours, lino prints and oil paints.

These seasonal paintings are Gordon's attempt to express his feelings for landscapes in their various guises.

Sussex Thaw   *Watercolour*

Schooled in the tradition of "English Watercolour", his artistic influences are widespread although not all are obvious at first glance.

Painters such as Charles Tunnicliffe, Andrew Wyeth, Stanley Badmin, Eric Ravilious, Richard Eurich and Charles Knight have all played their part and will continue to do so.

Gordon regards his output as "works in progress", a continuous learning process as he hones his skill in the search for fresh experiences and expressions.

"The biggest challenge is selecting what you want to paint," he explains. "I have to decide what I want to say about any particular subject and then interpret that into a painting rather than just paint the scene. With each painting you have to put something of yourself into the work." ■

Tillington sketch

Plaistow Morning   *Watercolour*

In Winter's Grip   *Watercolour*

VILLAGE LIFE

It's a scene that is quintessentially English. An expanse of grass in or near the centre of a village, perhaps a pond, an occasional tree and an overriding sense of peace and timelessness.

Depending on the season, an outdoor gathering of villagers at a fete or fair and, if space permits, a game of cricket or stoolball extending into the late evening.

The village green has played an important role in the everyday life of those who seek a more sedate pace of life away from concrete conurbations. Fortunately, aware

of the pressure on such prized recreational and social areas, the use of such greens by a significant number of residents "for lawful sports and pastimes for at least 20 years" is recognised as a right.

In earlier times the village green was usually a stretch of common grassland in or near a rural settlement and provided grazing and a pond for watering stock animals.

The game of cricket has particular significance in the Weald with historic evidence suggesting that the game was devised during Norman or Saxon times by children living there.

The Dog Show   *Watercolour*

Playing on grass kept short by grazing sheep it was possible to throw or "bowl" a bag of wool or rags at a target, usually the wicket gate of the animal enclosure, with the batsman using a stick or shepherd's crooked staff to defend the wicket.

Top left, above and below:
Best in the village show
Watercolour

His 'n Hers   *Watercolour*

The Builder's Shed, Chithurst   *Watercolour*

It is thought that cricket continued as primarily a children's game until the beginning of the 17th Century when the sport was increasingly played by adults.

Centuries later, it is significant that one of cricket's leading producers of bats for international players, Gray-Nicholls, is based at Robertsbridge in East Sussex.

World racquets champion H.J. Gray founded the racquet-making company H.J. Gray and Sons in 1855 and it later moved to the manufacture of cricket bats.

L.J. Nicholls had started making cricket bats in his workshop at Robertsbridge in 1876 and both companies became renowned for making bats for the leading players of the day. The outcome was a merger to form Gray-Nicolls in the 1940s.

Another game with its roots in the region is marbles and every Good Friday Tinsley Green, near Crawley, hosts the international marbles championship.

Teams from Europe, Japan, Australia and America have

Half Term   *Watercolour*

Evening Stoolball in the Weald   *Watercolour*

taken part in a tournament that was launched in 1932 but follows in the tradition of a game that dates back to 1588 when marbles was chosen as the deciding game of a sporting encounter between two suitors for the hand of a Tinsley Green milk maid.

In those more religious times, marbles was one of the few sports that could be played during Lent. As a result the contest was held every year on Good Friday

The related game of stoolball, sometimes called "cricket in the air", dates back to at least the 15th Century and was traditionally played by milkmaids using their milking stools as a "wicket".

A reference to "playing stoolball" appears in Shakespeare's tragicomedy "The Two Noble Kinsmen" in 1634 but it is believed the phrase is used as a euphemism for sexual behaviour referring to a time when the game was played for courtship purposes rather than a competitive event.

Stoolball is still popular in the Weald where teams, mostly comprising ladies, play regular league games. In addition to overseas fixtures, stoolball has also been played at Lord's cricket ground and in the gardens of Buckingham Palace. ■

On the Allotments, Liss   *Watercolour*

After the Storm   *Watercolour*

Our Vanishing Letterboxes and ....
Watercolour

.... Our Vanishing Phone Boxes
Watercolour

Over the River Rother   *Watercolour*

The Rich Soil of the Weald   *Watercolour*

HILAIRE BELLOC

The restorative qualities of the Weald are evident among those who have lived and worked or just visited an area that offers both calming and uplifting experiences. The author Hilaire Belloc was one of those to appreciate these qualities.

Although born in France, Belloc spent much of his boyhood at Slindon, Sussex, a move made largely on account of the infant Belloc's health.

His mother believed that the "pure, sweet air" of the Downs would keep her son free from the illnesses and epidemics that afflicted London where the family first settled.

Belloc's Mill, Shipley *Watercolour*

She was right and Hilaire's upbringing in the country produced a robust adult who became one of the most prolific writers in England.

Belloc achieved international recognition for his books and poems but it was whilst living, working and walking in the south that he developed a deep love for the Weald.

The Crown Inn, Chiddingfold
Watercolour

"I Never Get Between the Pines, But I Smell the Sussex Air"
Watercolour

It was in Shipley in West Sussex that Belloc bought land and a house to live in with his family. At Gumber Farm near Bignor there is a plaque to the writer along with the inscription "Lift up your hearts in Gumber".

His surroundings also instilled a deep affection for and interest in Sussex and its people and these influences can be found in poems such as "West Sussex Drinking Song", "The South Country" and "Ha'nacker Mill".

In "The South Country" Belloc refers to the men of the Sussex Weald as "the kindest and most wise" who "watch the stars from silent folds" and "stiffly plough the field".

On a lighter note in "West Sussex Drinking Song" he acknowledges that: "They sell good beer at Haslemere and at Little Cowfold a beggar may drink his fill".

Spring Afternoon, Treyford   *Watercolour*

Balls Cross on a Sunday Morning   *Watercolour*

THE PLOUGHING MATCH

Initially drawn by oxen, ploughs have been used in farming for most of recorded history. This basic tool may have been simple in its construction in the early days but it signifies one of the major advances in agriculture in order to satisfy the ever-increasing demand for food.

One Man and his Dog   *Watercolour*

The oxen were later replaced by horses and mules but in the more industrialised nations, mechanical means of pulling the plough started to emerge.

Steam-powered tractors were in turn superseded by the petrol or diesel-driven models and more modern and refined versions are now a common sight in our patchwork of fields.

Waiting for the Off   *Watercolour*

But the old techniques are not forgotten and as the old ploughman's song says: "We have all ploughed an acre, I swear and vow. And we are all jolly fellows that follow the plough".

Agricultural areas such as the Weald hold regular ploughing matches during the season bringing a nostalgic collection of man-operated, horse-drawn and tractor-pulled ploughs to a local farmer's fields.

Such events are a popular feature of country life when farming families and their working dogs meet interested members of the public to watch a contest where points are awarded not only for the straightness and neatness of the resulting furrows but for the condition of the soil in preparation for the sowing of the next crop. All done in carefully designated sections within a specified time.

It is estimated that more than 250 local ploughing societies are affiliated to The Society of Ploughmen which was founded in 1972. Modern day matches under

The Experts   *Watercolour*

the Society's auspices allow local entrants to progress from club events through to county finals and then the British National Ploughing Championships in Kent.

Two hundred and fifty top ploughmen competed in these national championships for two places in the 2016 World Ploughing Contest in York.

The Weald is well provided with ploughing match associations and during early Autumn most of the districts have their ploughing match fixtures.

Records show that such competitions in Sussex go back to 1797 when an important contest was held at Petworth. Rules for this meeting were that ploughmen should plough one statute acre of ground with two horses working in the shortest time and in the best manner.

The prize was two guineas for the best horse ploughman and went to John Blackman who completed his task in three hours and 53 minutes. ∎

Dad's Hat   *Watercolour*

RUDYARD KIPLING

Bateman's sketch *Watercolour*

A literary genius responsible for some of the world's best-known books, Rudyard Kipling described Sussex as "the most marvellous of all foreign countries that I have ever been in".

He was born in Bombay but moved at the age of five to England when he and his younger sister boarded with a couple at Southsea. He returned to India at the age of 16 to work as a newspaper reporter at the start of a literary career that was to take him to London, America, South Africa and Devon before settling eventually, at the age of 36, at Bateman's at Burwash, East Sussex.

By this time, Kipling had arguably become the most famous writer in the English-speaking world. But he was to enjoy more prolific years at "this good and peaceable place" in the richly wooded landscape of the Sussex Weald. In his autobiography, Kipling described Bateman's as: "A real house in which to settle down for keeps."

Oast and Dovecote, Bateman's *Watercolour*

Bateman's Beehives   *Watercolour*

The 17th Century house is built of local sandstone with the quarry from which the stones were cut being just across the lane from the garden gate. It was built by a Wealden ironmaster at a time when the Sussex Weald and its dense forests provided the charcoal for the burgeoning English iron industry. Terraced lawns leading to a walled garden of old red brick, two oast houses and an aged silver grey oak dovecote on top.

Fittingly the internal structures, staircase and panelling are all cut from local oak trees.

Bateman's is now a public museum dedicated to the author following his widow Carrie's bequest to the National Trust of the house, its estate of some 300 acres and a £5,000 endowment.

It was her wish that Kipling's study should remain undisturbed and some of the rooms be open for inspection. It was from this study that Kipling immersed himself in the life of Sussex, telling its history through the children's stories of "Puck of Pook's Hill" and creating a literary legacy from his observation of Sussex people and their traditions.

"The Blue Weald"   *Watercolour*

His "Sussex" poem captured this atmosphere and spirit referring to the "blunt, bow-headed, whale-backed Downs" and the "bare slopes where chasing shadows skim".

In this same poem Kipling refers to the "Blue goodness of the Weald" and this is a feature that many artists and photographers have attempted to capture as the landscape takes on the distinctive hue of an early morning sunrise.

References to local places abound in another of his poems, "The Run of the Downs" which starts with the observation that:" The Weald is good, the Downs are best" and ends with some local advice:

"The Downs are sheep, the Weald is corn
You be glad you are Sussex born."

In his time Kipling was one of the most popular writers in England being responsible for works of fiction such as "The Jungle Book" and "Kim" and many short stories including "The Man who would be King."

To this should be added a collection of poems including "Mandalay" and "The White Man's Burden". His prowess as a writer was recognised with the award of The Nobel Prize for Literature in 1907.

The boy from Bombay who went on to become one of the best known late Victorian poets and story tellers died in 1936 at the age of 70. ■

THE SUSSEX WEED

Winter Oak   *Watercolour & Oil Crayon*

So common were oak trees in Sussex that they were nicknamed the "Sussex Weed".

Indeed the county is still believed to be one of the most wooded parts of lowland Britain with the English oak being predominant in southern and central British broad-leaved woods.

Kipling's "Sussex" poem refers to: "Huge oaks and old, the which we hold. No more than Sussex weed."

With its matchless strength and resistance to rotting, the oak was a natural choice for buildings, fuel, charcoal and furniture.

One thing is certain, authentic Wealdsmen past and present have a loving and proprietorial relationship with the English oak.

Further afield, the oak has for centuries been a national symbol of strength and survival and has played an important part in our culture including being the traditional choice for the festive Yule log, to featuring on pound coins and being used as a symbol for environmental and community organisations. ■

March Moon, Didling   *Watercolour & Ink*

Quercus robur   *Watercolour*

FARMING IN THE WEALD

Sussex Wagon   *Pencil and Watercolour*

The densely wooded landscape does not give up its secrets lightly. But look through the trees and you will find a Weald landscape that, despite dramatic changes in farming and land management, still presents a picture of traditional practices.

In common with other rural areas, the Weald has experienced huge pressures as a result of changing consumer tastes, competition from cheaper imports and, more recently, a dramatic surge in land values.

Faced with such challenges the resilient and resolute farmers have stayed true to their traditions and still work in harmony with nature to produce their crops and raise livestock and have protected natural habitats and wildlife that have been wiped away by the mass production techniques in other parts of the UK.

Buckmoor Farm, Petersfield   *Watercolour*

And it has also been a case of making the most of a dubious hand that has been dealt by Mother Nature.

The infertile sands of the High Weald and the wet, sticky clays of the Low Weald are not suited to intensive arable farming. Also, the difficulties of working this land are intensified by the shape and steep features of these areas.

As a result, mixed farms offering land that provides grazing for animals and the opportunity to grow cereals, fruit and hops operate in the High Weald while the heavy soil of the Low Weald offers mostly grazing and hop growing.

Fordson Major, Sheet   *Watercolour*

Morning Light   *Watercolour*

The Weald has its own breed of cattle called the Sussex although these animals are as numerous in Kent and parts of Surrey.

And the abundance of oak trees – and their acorns – meant that pigs found a plentiful supply of food among the extensive woods.

Resourceful farmers have also looked for modern alternatives to traditional crops and there are vineyards producing high quality wine, the growth of medicinal and aromatic plants, plus a healthy interest in organic food production. ■

The Red Hat   *Watercolour*

The Old Cart Shed, Redford   *Watercolour*

HOPS AND VINES

Kentish Oasts   *Watercolour*

The long lines of hop poles and the distinctive funnel-shaped chimneys of the region's oast houses show that the essence of beer production is still alive although the number of hop gardens and breweries has decreased as the brewing operation has moved elsewhere.

Hops have been grown in the High Weald since the 16th Century when Flemish weavers, attracted by the Kent wool industry, settled in the area and introduced perennial hop plants.

The settlers' predilection was for a bitter flavoured beer rather than the sweeter variety of the English ale which was made just with malt and water. The taste and superior preservative qualities meant that

Humulus lupulus

Vineyard

hopped ale or beer became so popular that hop gardens, oasthouses and breweries flourished to meet the demand.

Most of the commercial production of hops has migrated elsewhere and many of the oasthouses have been converted to residential use.

But the distinctive taste of hopped ale remains a firm favourite with beer drinkers everywhere.

The warm climate and south-facing chalky slopes of the Weald make it ideal for the production of wines that are attracting global recognition.

In the early days of the area's move into viticulture, growers used little known grape varieties and production methods that suited a colder climate. But as the UK has become warmer and drier, Weald vineyards have been able to make more wines of greater appeal using more familiar and better known grape varieties.

So great has this improvement been that Weald-produced wines have won international awards and the area is recognised as a wine-producing region of distinction. ■

Chardonnay Grapes

THE IRON INDUSTRY

Wealden Ironworks c.1600   *Watercolour and Gouache*

Little remains of an industry that dates back to prehistoric times when iron was produced in the Weald using small clay kilns called bloomeries.

In Roman times the Weald became one of the most important iron producing areas in Britain. But the end of Roman rule marked a decline in iron smelting until changes in production methods and the need to provide munitions meant that the Weald, once again, became the cradle of iron making during the 16th Century. Iron production was to reach its peak during the Civil War to meet the need for weapons and ammunition.

The blast furnace was in general use in Europe before Henry VIII initiated the casting of cannon in England as part of his plan to create a stronger Navy. English iron workers rose to the challenge and used blast furnaces to produce cast iron cannon. One of the first furnaces at Newbridge in Ashdown Forest is regarded as the birthplace of the British iron industry.

Further blast furnaces and gun foundaries in and around the forest led to a production process that included a breakthrough in the casting of cannon and even greater prosperity in the region.

It's hard to imagine how such an intrusive operation involving heat, water and other natural elements such as ore, clay, sandstone and timber could be masked within today's landscape of small fields, dense woodlands and steep valleys.

But remote signposts to places such as Hammer Pond House, Black Hill, Furnace Pond, Hammer Hill Wood and Cinder Bank are clues to when the High Weald of Kent and Sussex and adjacent parts of Surrey and Hampshire were the centre of England's iron industry.

Less obvious are the tranquil, tree-lined lakes and ponds with an abundance of waterfowl and other wildlife that hide within their watery depths most of the brick and metalwork that formed hammer ponds to feed the forges.

The convenience of raw materials such as heat-resistant clay, later replaced by sandstone to build furnace hearths, the ample supply of wood to make charcoal for fuel and the quality of local ore were fundamental to local iron making.

Add to this the many swift streams in deep wooded valleys known to locals as "ghylls" that provided the water for cooling the iron and, later when heads of water were created, to turn waterwheels to power furnace bellows and drive huge forge hammers to pound pig iron into refined bars.

It is reported that in the 13th Century the Weald had replaced the Forest of Dean as the main source of iron goods for London and the south.

But the most rapid growth of industry came in the 16th Century with the peak of production during Elizabethan times when it was estimated that a half

Iron Objects from Haslemere Educational Museum   *Watercolour*

The Blacksmith's Art   *Watercolour*

of the iron mills in the country were in Sussex and Surrey.

Within 50 years a decline had set in but local production continued into the 18th Century with a significant loss for Sussex in 1769 of the Naval contract for cannon and shot.

The rapid decline of the industry was attributed to the exhaustion of the woodland from which the charcoal fuel was obtained. But it is more likely that the demise followed the successful application of coal to iron smelting and the inevitable movement of the industry to the coalfields.

Cannon Power

Sussex iron masters led the way in the production of guns, not only for England's armed forces but also for the armies and navies of other countries.

Records show that the first English cannon to be cast in one piece was at an iron smelting centre at Buxted in 1543. The iron master responsible for this achievement was Ralph Hogge (or Hog) and the deeds of his house record the following: "In this house lived Ralph Hog who at the furnace at Buxted cast the first cannon in England."

Cities such as Birmingham, Sheffield and Newcastle would later take over as major production centres but at the time of the Spanish Armada in 1588 the Weald was a major source of iron, increasingly used for the production of cannon.

Fortunately for the English Navy, according to some reports, the Weald-produced cast iron cannon had an important advantage over the bronze and brass guns of the Spanish fleet. The Sussex cannon could be fired repeatedly whereas, after firing a few rounds, the Spanish artillerymen had to stop to let their guns cool.

Whether it was superior firepower or better seamanship on the part of Sir Francis Drake and his men, the Spanish Armada was harried along the south coast to the Isle of Wight and then Selsey Bill before eventually setting sail for Calais.

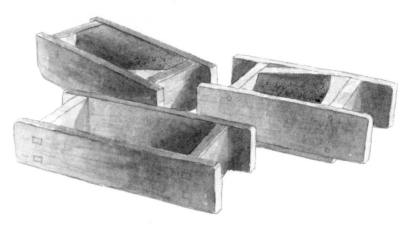

Brick Moulds   *Watercolour*

Brick Making

Another industry to make use of natural resources is brick building and, unlike the iron forges, continues to operate commercially in the Weald.

Many villages and small hamlets provide living evidence of the use of Wealden clays to make house bricks. Even today there are local companies carrying on this tradition and, in particular, the distinctive Sussex Sandstone, in addition to being used for hundreds of years, can be seen in use on restoration and new build properties.

A part of the process of making these bricks involved leaving them in drying sheds before the freshly moulded bricks were fired in a kiln. One of these drying sheds, now re-erected at the Weald and Downland Museum, was built in 1733 near Petersfield but had to be closed down early in the Second World War because it was feared the glow from the open-topped kiln would be a landmark for enemy aircraft.

Further evidence of the Weald's brickmaking industry is provided by the presence of ponds formed naturally once clay had been dug out to obtain the raw ingredient for an industry which still operates today. ■

Wealden Cannon from Royal Armouries   *Watercolour*

Brick Drying Shed   *Watercolour*

'MAD JACK' FULLER

Characters abound within the Weald and none more so than "Mad Jack" Fuller or "Honest John" as he preferred to be called.

One of the great English eccentrics, John Fuller was born at North Stoneham in Hampshire, and in 1777 at the age of 20 he inherited the Sussex estates and Jamaican plantations of his uncle, the MP Rose Fuller.

This included the Rose Hill estate, now Brightling Park in East Sussex from where his military and political career developed. He was a captain of a light infantry company in the Sussex Militia,

was appointed the High Sheriff of Sussex in 1796 followed by an appointment as a captain in the Sussex Gentlemen and Yeomanry Cavalry.

But at the age of 23, his thoughts turned to politics and he was elected a Member of Parliament for Southampton and later for Sussex.

However, his liking for the demon drink led to his involvement in an incident in 1810 with the Speaker of Parliament which resulted in his seizure by the Sergeant at Arms and public disgrace.

He retired from politics two years later but his public work continued as the Squire of Brightling and he became well known as a builder of follies, a philanthropist and patron of the arts and sciences.

Bodiam sketch *Watercolour*

Mad Jack's Pyramid, Brightling   *Watercolour*

He purchased and commissioned many paintings from JMW Turner and was also a sponsor and mentor to Michael Faraday, the British 19th Century inventor and electrical pioneer.

The collection of follies he established in the area was impressive and included Brightling Needle, a 65ft high obelisk that some sources claim was erected to commemorate Nelson's victory at Trafalgar in 1805; The Temple in the grounds of Brightling Park built to resemble a Greek temple; The Observatory which was equipped with expensive equipment including a Camera Obscura; and The Watch Tower, believed

Bodiam Castle   *Watercolour*

to have been built to enable Fuller to watch the restoration of Bodiam Castle.

In 1828 he financed the building of the Belle Tout lighthouse on the cliff at Beachy Head in East Sussex and a year later he bought Bodiam Castle for 3000 guineas at an auction to save it from being dismantled.

He also had a conical-shaped building, referred to as The Pyramid erected in the churchyard of St Thomas a Becket in Brightling as a mausoleum.

According to local legend, following his death in 1834 at the age of 77, Fuller was buried seated within the pyramid, holding a bottle of claret. However, when the monument was opened in 1982 during renovations, it proved to be empty. ■

WEALDEN CHURCHES

The Weald is dotted with ancient churches, many dating to before the Norman conquest. Some are hidden away in the wooded hills whilst others provide a visual focus in open country.

Early Wealden churches were often half-timbered buildings built in the traditional vernacular style. But increasing prosperity led to extensive rebuilding to accommodate a growing population and larger, wealthier congregations.

As a result, dating the early religious buildings is often difficult because of the changes brought about by new rulers. This part of the south of England, for instance, was heavily influenced by trade, religious practices and architectural styles from France well before 1066.

Many of the churches appear to have grown organically having become an integral part of the very fabric of the land.

A perfect example of this is St Thomas à Becket at Fairfield on Romney Marsh. Its isolated setting amongst water channels, reed beds and grazing sheep is an artist's dream, transforming this otherwise featureless, windswept marsh.

In contrast, hidden above the River Rother in West Sussex is St Mary's at Chithurst. This gem is found at the last moment, on a mound surrounded by trees and giant cow parsley.

It's regarded as a simple country church but the late 11th Century building hides a dark secret. History comes alive here as visitors learn that the Rector, the Reverend John Denham, was stabbed and murdered

St Thomas à Becket, Fairfield   *Watercolour*

while walking home from Stedham on a December evening in 1757. His murderer was tried, convicted and hanged at Horsham.

But no reason for the crime is proffered. Why was the rector killed? For money? For revenge? Who knows? Possibly the only person who could shed any light on the crime was the murderer himself, a man called Aps. But he gave no explanation before being hung

St Mary's, Chithurst   *Watercolour*

The Holly and the Ivy, St Botolph's, Hardham   *Watercolour*

"without the least sign of repentance." Something to ponder while crossing the same fields today.

Church architectural styles vary greatly in the Weald from structures little more than chapels such as Chithurst to sturdy buildings with solid towers like, once more, St Thomas à Becket, this time at Capel in Kent. Thomas à Becket is reputed to

have preached here, maybe he preached at other churches now named after him including Brightling in East Sussex.

It is pure coincidence that Gordon chose to paint three churches for this book, each with the same saint's name. Could this be due to the Weald's proximity to Canterbury where the saint and martyr

Three wall painting fragments from St Botolph's, Hardham, including "Adam and Eve"
Watercolour

was Archbishop from 1162 until his murder by followers of King Henry II in the cathedral in 1170?

A painting of the churchyard steps at Brightling is included because, as is often the case, the environs of churches convey a mood and sense of the passage of time.

Steps and flagstones worn by thousands of feet over centuries; leaning gravestones, eroded by wind, rain and frost but still displaying ghost images of names along with cherub's heads and skulls; the cracking ivy-and lichen-covered tombs, some surrounded by iron railings. And over all, the ancient yew trees, a reminder of our pagan past and longbows at Agincourt.

The Weald is not rich in grand cathedral-like churches as found in East Anglia with its prosperous

wool churches but instead offers intimate places where people can still worship, sitting in the same pews as have congregations for centuries.

These humble, quiet, gathering places are the very essence of our Weald.

Some Wealden churches rely on the work of itinerant groups of workshop artists rather than master stone or timber craftsmen for their place in religious history.

Unlike more modern places of worship, pre-reformation churches used highly decorative wall paintings to tell graphic biblical stories in a way that a largely illiterate population could understand.

Although on the South Downs, Coombes Church (right) has this wonderful painted figure holding up an arch
Watercolour

Much of this imagery was later eradicated but Mary Tudor's attempts to re-establish Catholicism included replacing or restoring works that had been damaged or removed.

Many wall paintings were lost under coatings of whitewash but some survived behind the covering of paint and careful restorers were able to bring these hidden stories back to life.

One of the best examples of this Romanesque style of painting is the small church of St Botolph's at Hardham in Sussex.

The wall paintings here date back to the beginning of the 12th Century and are considered to be England's earliest mediaeval frescoes.

It is thought that groups of travelling artists, perhaps based at the Cluniac Priory in Lewes or Chichester, created the works at Hardham and were responsible for similar paintings within the five Lewes Group of Churches that included St John the Baptist Church at Clayton, the Church of St Michael at Plumpton, and Coombes near Lancing.

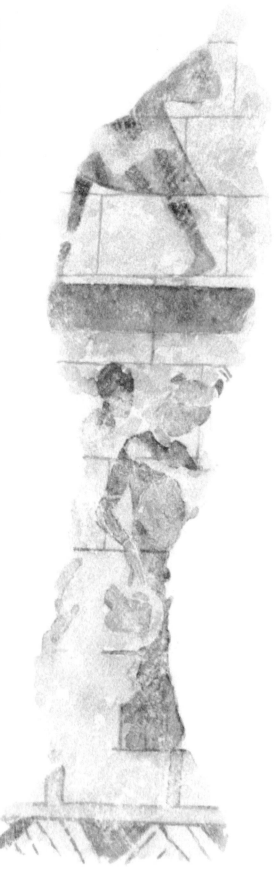

St Thomas à Becket, Capel, and a fragment of one of its frescos
Watercolour

Churchyard Steps, Brightling   *Watercolour*

The Cokelers

As traditional mainstream religions flourished, the rural population was also becoming involved in non-conformist worship that appealed more to the poor in urban and rural areas.

Fundamentalist religious sects became extremely popular and the Weald saw the arrival of the Society of Dependants when shoemaker turned preacher John Sirgood arrived at Loxwood in West Sussex in 1850 after he walked the 40 odd miles from Clapham with his wife, Harriett, pushing a handcart.

Sirgood's fame spread as he started to preach to the poor and, despite opposition from local landowners and clergy, he formed his own religious sect, named the Dependants or, more informally, the Cokelers.

His followers adhered to a strict code of conduct including no secular music, books, games or tobacco. Alcohol was also forbidden and it is believed that the local name of Cokelers came from their habit of drinking cocoa after meetings.

Although marriage was not forbidden, it was not part of their doctrine. The Dependants believed that those seeking a "higher life" should remain single with no need for earthly institutions such as marriage. But it was also alleged that the name Cokelers is a corruption of Cuckolders when their opponents accused the Dependants of "going about with other men's wives".

Nevertheless, Sirgood developed a substantial following through open-air meetings or in the homes of his followers. He offered salvation for the poor, an emphasis on valuing poverty and humility and total rejection of the affluence and indulgence of the society in which they lived and worshipped.

His followers set up the Combination Stores in Loxwood and ran the business as a co-operative selling produce from their own farms.

The stores no longer trade but the building still exists.

By the time of Sirgood's death in 1885 it was estimated there were around 2,000 Dependants but interest in the sect started to decline and by 1990 only a few elderly followers remained. ■

THE UCKFIELD MARTYR

The Uckfield Union workhouse no longer exists – housing now occupies the site to the south of the town in East Sussex. But nearly two centuries later, the story of George Wren offers an insight into how the odds in Victorian times were stacked against a child of the workhouse.

Suspicion fell upon poor Wren after a hayrick near the workhouse was set alight on 8th November 1832. Despite protesting his innocence and being seen trying to douse the blaze with buckets of water, he was convicted by what was described as a "meager case" with a distinct lack of evidence.

Pleas for clemency based on the fact that he was only 19 were ignored and at the end of the trial at the Winter Assizes at Lewes, Wren was sentenced to death.

So on 5th January 1833 a large crowd assembled in front of Horsham Gaol to witness the execution. Speaking with a hangman's noose around his neck, Wren protested his innocence. "I have been condemned by the people of Uckfield" he proclaimed.

"Fare you all well" were his final words before the noose tightened.

It was reported that many in the crowd were not convinced that justice was being done and that even if Wren were guilty, the sentence was too severe.

The strongest evidence linking Wren with the hayrick fire was an imprint of his left boot found at the scene.

A few years later, a man on his deathbed in Brighton confessed that he had set fire to the hayrick and had worn George's boots to do so.

By then, with no friend or family to claim his body, the bones of poor George Wren in a corner grave of the old churchyard were the only earthly reminders of someone who never had the chance to "tread the straight path towards good citizenship". ■

Uckfield Workhouse   *Watercolour*

TIMBER, TILE & THATCH

Tile Hung Cottage, Wisborough Green
Watercolour

Weatherboarding   *Watercolour*

Horsham Stone Roofing
Watercolour

Oak Framing   *Watercolour*

Long before roads, canals and railways transformed the movement of heavy goods, local quarries, brickyards and sawmills provided the main source of building materials in the Weald.

Over time, this rich and abundant variety of raw materials was to influence many different building styles.

What is fascinating as you travel through the countryside between the Downs is how many villages, let alone towns, contain the full range of architectural styles.

Weatherboarding is not restricted to just parts of Kent; Oak framing appears throughout the area; Horsham stone is found in many places; and thatch, although rarer, appears too.

Obviously as earlier structures became uninhabitable and people prospered, new buildings of different styles and materials took their place.

The buildings illustrated on these two pages can all be found in one village, Wisborough Green, and they all fringe the green. But there is equal variety in terms of building styles beyond the centre of what was predominantly a farming community which was also rich in timber resources.

This surprising variety is perhaps not only due to the growing prosperity of people in the Weald but also to

Tile, Board and Staddle Stone Granary, Northchapel   *Watercolour*

current trends in house building and improved access to different raw materials.

Certainly the stone-built structures such as churches, manor houses or larger cottages have been financed by the more wealthy and were built to last. And, of course, they have.

All as a result of readily available resources and rural industries that have given rise to and supported local craftsmen and builders.

Much of the undoubted charm of the Wealden villages and older town centres is due to their patchwork of buildings. Buildings that often lean this way and that, structurally imperfect but visually impressive and memorable.

So many textures, surfaces, colours and shapes, all coming together to give what is ultimately an exciting but comforting, almost homely, feeling. ◼

Bayleaf Wealden Hall House from Chiddingstone, now re-erected at the Weald & Downland Open Air Museum   *Watercolour*

Frosty Morning, Stroud   *Oils*

Cowfold Thatch, Weald & Downland Open Air Museum   *Watercolour*

GREEN TUNNELS

The Weald's network of green tunnels provides popular reference points for artists of all abilities, from professional to weekend painters of pastoral scenes.

Maps of Roman roads and tracks suggest an integrated system of green routes that were mostly local in their use as drovers' roads, ridgeways or ancient trackways. Progressive

means of travel led to a breakdown of any formal system but the determined explorer can still find many of these natural routes.

In the winter these arteries are simply green tracks with high hedges and filled with small branches that have been cut or broken off. But when the hedges and trees on either side burst forth into their warm weather covering, the tracks become tunnels as nature forms a canopy to envelop the traveller.

No modern surface interferes with these timeless features and lush vegetation frequently takes over at ground level where the green lane is not used regularly.

The ever-changing moods created by these natural features are of particular interest to artists and photographers. On a still day the tunnels create a warm place of rest and reflection, free of noise and disturbance. However, the slightest breeze can suddenly spark a glitter ball of shadows and reflections as the sun's rays are transformed by an unseen force. ■

From the Weald to the Downs   *Watercolour*

THE WOODSMEN

It is a scene that has changed little over the centuries. Smoke from a wood fire rising through the dappled canopy as the woodsman prepares for a lengthy wait under a makeshift cover stretched between two trees.

Today's charcoal burner has some modern equipment to help make a living but the principle of making charcoal and the need to pass days while the burn took effect have not changed since production fuelled the Wealden ironworks in the 16th Century.

Summer Shelter   *Watercolour sketch*

Instead of mounds created by timber frames, whatever straw or herbage was to hand and covered with ashes and earth, today's charcoal burner uses a steel ring kiln to give the controlled burn that turns timber into charcoal.

The aim is to burn wood in a controlled way so that insufficient oxygen prevents complete combustion.

The biggest change, however, is that once burning charcoal used to be a major part of producers' lives. They lived for making charcoal. It gave them a place to live and a livelihood and they also lived off the land where they made charcoal.

Nowadays, people involved in charcoal burning have other jobs such as conservation, coppicing, tree surgery and other related sources of income. Charcoal has become an add-on to their daily lives. We see more woodsmen and conservationists than charcoal burners.

Coming to the Boil   *Watercolour*

Charcoal Burning in the Surrey Woods   *Watercolour*

It's ironic that modern-day charcoal burners now talk in terms of woodland management and the preservation of the countryside and the wildlife when their forbearers felled so many trees in their quest for fuelling the ancient forges that acts of parliament had to be passed to regulate and prohibit the felling of trees for charcoal manufacture.

Before World War 1 charcoal burners had dwindled to a mere handful. Cheap imported charcoal and inhospitable working conditions resulted in a major

Burning Brush   *Watercolour*

It can also be used as a soil fertiliser to replace pesticides that can have a damaging effect on wildlife and water supplies.

Nowadays charcoal is mass produced in sophisticated retorts. It continues to be used in modern industry but the days of the smoke-blackened men, wise in the ways of the wood, are largely over.

The Sussex Trug

The Sussex trug is a basket made of split oak designed to carry a wide variety of produce. Its name is derived from "trog" an Anglo Saxon term for a wooden vessel – the basket being boat-shaped.

Used primarily for holding garden produce it has a handle and rim of coppiced sweet chestnut wood and a body of thin boards of willow.

They were probably originated in Sussex because of the abundance of chestnut coppice and willows found on the marshes. Gradually the shapes and sizes of these distinctive baskets became standardised with the best known being the common or garden trug. However, there is a diverse range of traditional trugs from garden and oval trugs to the more specialised "large log" and "walking stick" trugs.

reduction of charcoal burning but the outbreak of hostilities in 1914 provided a sudden boost for the industry.

Gas warfare in the trenches created an urgent need for protection of the troops and they were issued with respirators containing charcoal, a powerful absorbent of hazardous chemicals.

Which brings us back to the modern day charcoal burner with his passion for charcoal production and how it can be used to clean up pollution. With its neutral PH, charcoal is effective in water filters, masks and can be used to "sweeten" or cleanse water courses.

Witches' Brooms

The making of besoms or witches' brooms was popular in the south of England where birch coppices abounded.

Besom brooms are made from the twiggy growth of the birch tree and their production is regarded as a work of art by a country craftsperson.

Although hardly used any longer for practical purposes, the production continues to provide props for the makers of films such as Harry Potter and to supply shops and museums that operate in the world of witchcraft.

One Hampshire besom broom family company was awarded the Queen's Royal Warrant in 1999 making them the official broom makers for Buckingham Palace.

Pagan weddings also feature besom brooms where guests jump over the broomstick as part of the ceremony.

Glass Making

Little evidence can be found in the Weald of glass making despite the fact that small family-run concerns took advantage of the availability of large quantities of wood fuel and sand to make glass.

A process that was initially limited to the small scale production of forest glass for windows and vessels grew rapidly in the mid 16th Century.

Ample supplies of beech, preferred for melting glass because of its greater heating effect, were available in the Kirdford and Chiddingfold areas, whilst the main ingredient, sand, was obtained locally on the Folkstone and Hythe beds.

Approval from the Crown led to larger scale production whilst the influence of immigrant glass makers from Europe during the 16th Century led to

better quality glass as a result of changes in furnace technology and raw materials.

But the insatiable need for timber to feed the glass or iron works was to lead to a Royal Proclamation in 1615 which prohibited the burning of wood fuel for glass making, some three years after technical advances enabled the use of coal as a fuel in place of wood.

The last wood-fired furnace closed in 1618 but a fitting memorial to a once popular Wealden industry can be found at Chiddingfold and Kirdford churches where windows are glazed with fragments of glass uncovered by archaeologists who have dug former sites.

Chestnut Splitting Camp, Iping   *Watercolour*

Coppicing

Coppicing is one of the most fundamental of woodland crafts having been practised in British woodlands for centuries. It uses the principle that nature responds in a generous way to practices that preserve and promote regeneration and regrowth.

Cut almost any hardwood tree just above ground level and within a relatively short space of time shoots will develop to create the start of several trees where once there was just one.

By rotating the process, a woodsman can ensure a steady supply of natural and regenerated timber for a wide variety of uses in a sustainable way. ■

Tools of the Trade   *Watercolour*

FLORA & FAUNA

It was Satish Kumar, who warned the world that: "Without the land, the rivers, the oceans, the forests, the sunshine, the minerals and thousands of natural resources we would have no economy whatsoever."

No doubt the editor of The Ecologist & Resurgence magazine would have added that, given the above scenario, there would also not be any plants or animals.

I met the former monk, peace campaigner and environmental activist at an event in West Sussex and realised that his stark warning from 2008 is even more relevant to areas such as the Weald today.

In an area offering a greater than average variety of habitats for flora and fauna, the prospect of "fracking" in search oil and shale gas looms over the Weald Basin.

Opponents of this method of drilling predict it will have a devastating effect on the landscape, water supplies and wildlife.

The High Weald, with its ancient landscape of undulating hills, meadows and heathland is home to a number of rare species such as the dormouse, the orange and black pearl bordered fritillary butterfly and the black-headed cardinal beetle.

It also has a coastline of shingle ridges, brackish lagoons and marshland that supports wintering waterfowl including lapwings and reed warblers.

Within the numerous ponds, many the result of previous industrial activity described elsewhere in this book, can be found rare great crested newts and uncommon water beetles while the fast-flowing ghyll streams are ideal for brown trout, bullhead and the endangered sea trout.

A heavy clay soil and steep slopes in this part of the Weald mean that many ancient meadows and roadside verges are undisturbed with the result that different types of grasses and wildflowers, along with rare orchid species, can be found.

The Low Weald is much less wooded than the High Weald and, being more low lying features several mill and hammer ponds, streams and rivers.

Water voles once thrived in this aquatic setting but it is now thought that numbers of this rodent, immortalised by Ratty from "Wind in the Willows", have declined by a fifth in the UK since 2011.

Woodlands, wetlands and unimproved grassland create their own familiar landscapes of bluebells and primroses but rarities such as the spiked campion and coralroot can still be found.

The same habitats encourage the greatest gathering of bird species in the Low Weald including nightingales, kingfishers, lapwing, snipe, reed and sedge warblers.

The mix of woods, pastures and wetlands create good feeding grounds for bats, including the rare and protected barbastelle bats that roost in the woodlands and then search for food in the wet grassland on a nightly basis.

It is believed that the Weald harbours the largest population of feral wild boar in the UK. The wild boar became extinct in Britain 300 years ago but

Magpie on our Plums   *Watercolour*

following escapes from boar farms and deliberate releases, numbers of this ancestor of most domestic pig breeds are rising.

Famed for its speed whilst chasing prey – it can reach 200 mph during a hunting stoop or dive – peregrine falcons were extinct in Sussex between 1945 and 1990. But the bird nicknamed "the eagle of the South Country" has now returned to both rural sites as well as nesting in urban environments such as Chichester Cathedral and Brighton.

This highly-selective snapshot of The Weald's flora and fauna began with a warning from an eminent enivironmentalist. It ends with a reference to a pioneering naturalist and ornithologist whose work in the 18th Century is credited with shaping the modern attitude of respect for nature.

From his home in Selborne on the western tip of The Weald, Gilbert White, based his meticulous studies on personal observations gained from walking the fields near his Hampshire home and a number of journeys within Britain.

His seminal work "The Natural History of Selborne" could only hope to capture some of the huge number of species and variety of plants and animals.

As well as looking he listened to what was going on around him and, based largely on their songs, he was able to identify the three species of willow wren – chiffchaff, willow warbler and wood warbler.

White acknowledged the role played by all creatures – great or small – and in a specific reference to the earthworm he wrote:" ….. 'though in appearance a small and despicable link in the chain of nature, yet, if lost, would make a lamentable chasms. Worms seem to be the great promoters of vegetation, which would proceed lamely without them"

He also commented on shell-less snails, or slugs as they are known, "which silently and imperceptibly make amazing 'havock' in the field or garden."

Long may the flora and fauna of the Weald continue to amaze. ■

Dawn Patrol   *Watercolour and Pastel*

Into the Light   *Watercolour*

Two of a Kind, Dungeness *Watercolour*

It's an area of extreme contrasts. A natural creation of one of the largest shingle banks which is also home to the polar opposite of natural energy production, a couple of nuclear reactors.

A smattering of sparse vegetation including occasional flashes of colour from wild flowers provide delights in a sterile landscape battered by waves and wind in equal measure.

Such desolation may deter all but the hardiest of visitors but this remoteness encourages wildlife in

Remote Dungeness   *Watercolour*

many forms and Dungeness is a protected area for birds, unusual plants and rare invertebrates.

Such dramatic scenery also attracts those seeking inspiration for their work as writers, artists, designers and even film directors. The late radical filmmaker Derek Jarman made his home here in a tarred black fisherman's cottage and used the weather-beaten landscape as the setting for his film "The Last of England".

Dungeness sits on the edge of Romney Marsh at the southern-most point in Kent with the French coastline just 30 miles across the water.

Despite the vast expanse of shingle beach, believed to be the largest of its type in Europe, it's difficult to overlook the foreboding presence of the two nuclear power stations that dominate the landscape. One reactor was closed at the end of 2006 but the other is to stay open until 2028 after a review by owners EDF.

There has been a beacon of light at Dungeness Point since the 17th Century although only two of the five lighthouses erected at Dungeness have survived, one of which is in use today.

At the southern tip is an intriguing collection of black tarred fishermen's huts, mainly built around old railway carriages, that were constructed before the days of planning permission. Some are

still occupied by local fishermen but others have become the quirky homes of those looking for seclusion and a traditional way of living.

Rather appropriately, Dungeness is the end of the line for The Romney, Hythe and Dymchurch Railway, at 15-inch gauge, one of the world's smallest independent railways. The service operates most of the year providing a link for the local community as well as being a popular tourist attraction during the warmer months.

Despite being one of the driest areas of the United Kingdom – it is officially designated a desert –

Dungeness is a haven for wild flowers and wildlife.

The stark shingle landscape creates a uniquely important ecological site with flora and fauna that is special to its surroundings. In addition to a large Royal Society for the Protection of Birds site, the reserve has special protection status because of the many unusual plants, rare invertebrates and birdlife.

It has been said that Dungeness is like Marmite, you either love it or hate it. The stark wild beauty and distinctive character of this shingle desert engenders feelings of awe, wonder and curiosity in equal measure. ■

References

Sussex County Magazine

Journey through the Weald, Ben Darby, Robert Hale Ltd

The Kent and Sussex Weald, Peter Brandon, Phillimore

Weald of Kent and Sussex, Sheila Kaye-Smith, Robert Hale and Co

The Weald, S W Wooldridge and Frederick Goldring, Collins

Hammer and Furnace Ponds, Helen Pearce, Pomegranate Press

The Forgotten Arts, John Seymour, Dorling Kindersley

The South Country, Edward Thomas, Little Toller Books

Complete Verse, Hilaire Belloc, Pimlico

Bateman's, National Trust

Bodiam Castle, National Trust

The Forgotten Arts, John Seymour, The National Trust

The Haslemere Educational Museum, Haslemere, Surrey

The Illustrated Natural History of Selborne, Gilbert White, Webb & Bower

The High Weald Area of Outstanding Natural Beauty Unit

John Sirgood's Way, Peter Jerrome, Window Press

Our thanks for their support, advice and input to:

Haslemere Educational Museum

Weald & Downland Open Air Museum

West Sussex Record Office

Royal Armouries

Paul Wooldridge, gardener extraordinaire

Iain Plumer, charcoal burner

The ladies of Elsted Stoolball Club

End of the Day   *Watercolour*